NORTH AMERICAN ANIMALS

Wolverines

by Betsy Rathburn

BLASTOFF! READERS
3

BELLWETHER MEDIA • MINNEAPOLIS, MN

Note to Librarians, Teachers, and Parents:

Blastoff! Readers are carefully developed by literacy experts and combine standards-based content with developmentally appropriate text.

Level 1 provides the most support through repetition of high-frequency words, light text, predictable sentence patterns, and strong visual support.

Level 2 offers early readers a bit more challenge through varied simple sentences, increased text load, and less repetition of high-frequency words.

Level 3 advances early-fluent readers toward fluency through increased text and concept load, less reliance on visuals, longer sentences, and more literary language.

Level 4 builds reading stamina by providing more text per page, increased use of punctuation, greater variation in sentence patterns, and increasingly challenging vocabulary.

Level 5 encourages children to move from "learning to read" to "reading to learn" by providing even more text, varied writing styles, and less familiar topics.

Whichever book is right for your reader, Blastoff! Readers are the perfect books to build confidence and encourage a love of reading that will last a lifetime!

This edition first published in 2018 by Bellwether Media, Inc.

No part of this publication may be reproduced in whole or in part without written permission of the publisher. For information regarding permission, write to Bellwether Media, Inc., Attention: Permissions Department, 5357 Penn Avenue South, Minneapolis, MN 55419.

Library of Congress Cataloging-in-Publication Data

Names: Rathburn, Betsy, author.
Title: Wolverines / by Betsy Rathburn.
Other titles: Blastoff! Readers. 3, North American Animals.
Description: Minneapolis, MN : Bellwether Media, Inc., [2018] | Series: Blastoff! Readers: North American Animals | Audience: Ages 5-8. | Audience: K to Grade 3. | Includes bibliographical references and index.
Identifiers: LCCN 2017028797 | ISBN 9781626177314 (hardcover : alk. paper) | ISBN 9781681034720 (ebook)
Subjects: LCSH: Wolverine–Juvenile literature.
Classification: LCC QL737.C25 R39 2018 | DDC 599.76/6–dc23
LC record available at https://lccn.loc.gov/2017028797

Editor: Rebecca Sabelko   Designer: Josh Brink

Printed in the United States of America, North Mankato, MN.

Table of Contents

Wolverines are **solitary** animals not often seen by humans.

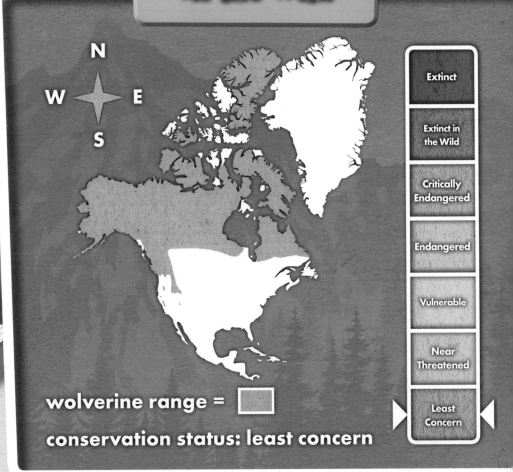

N
W E
S

wolverine range =

conservation status: least concern

Extinct

Extinct in
the Wild

Critically
Endangered

Endangered

Vulnerable

Near
Threatened

Least
Concern

These **mammals** are found
from Alaska to northeastern
Canada. Small numbers also
live in the **Pacific Northwest**.

Wolverines like to live in cold **climates**. Many make their homes in the **Arctic**.

They are often found in **bogs** and thick northern forests.

These animals do not stay in one place for long. They prowl the **tundra** in search of food.

Wolverines travel through
huge home ranges. These can
be hundreds of miles across!

Dressed for Cold Weather

Wolverines have thick fur
to keep them warm in cold
weather. Most of their fur is
dark brown or black.

Identify a Wolverine

short legs

light brown stripes

sharp claws

They have stripes of lighter brown fur on their heads. These stripes also run down each side of their bodies.

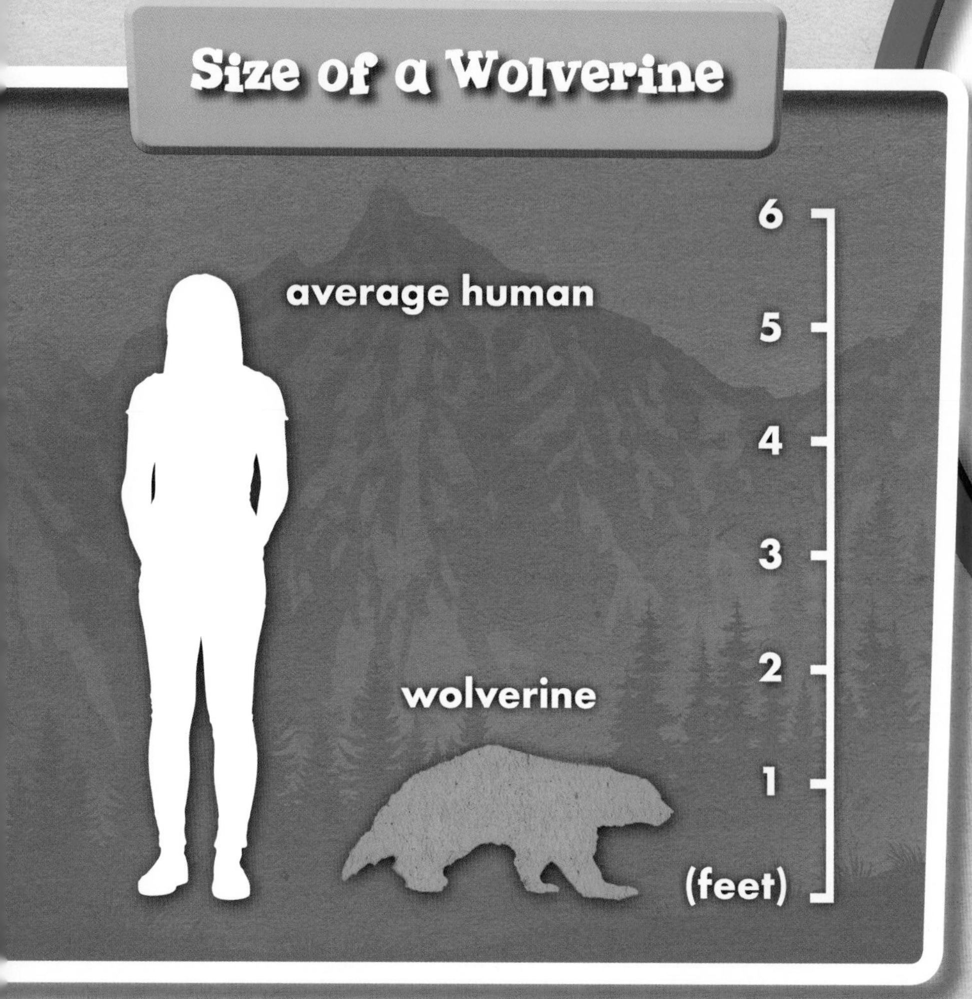

Size of a Wolverine

average human

wolverine

6
5
4
3
2
1
(feet)

Wolverines are one of the largest members of the weasel family. They grow up to 3.2 feet (1 meter) long.

Short legs and wide feet help
wolverines walk in deep snow.

Fearless Fighters

Adult wolverines have few **predators**. They can fight off animals many times their size.

These fearless fighters have sharp claws and strong teeth. They use these to **slash** enemies.

Wolverines are **scavengers**. They often take food other animals have killed. Favorite meals include deer, elk, and **rodents**.

elk

white-tailed deer

red squirrels

snowshoe hares

Sometimes, these **carnivores** hunt their own food. If there are leftovers, wolverines dig holes to store them for later.

Wolverine Kits

Every two years, female wolverines dig snow **dens**. They give birth inside these dens in late winter or early spring. Up to five **kits** are born in each litter. The kits **nurse** in the den for about three months.

Baby Facts

Name for babies:	kits
Size of litter:	1 to 5 kits
Length of pregnancy:	up to 9 months
Time spent with mom:	up to 2 years

When kits leave the den, they learn to find food. They stay with their mom until fall.

Then, wolverines are
ready to discover their
snowy surroundings!

Glossary

Arctic—the cold region around the North Pole

bogs—wet, spongy lands made up of dead plant material

carnivores—animals that only eat meat

climates—the specific weather conditions for certain areas

dens—sheltered places

kits—baby wolverines

mammals—warm-blooded animals that have backbones and feed their young milk

nurse—to drink mom's milk

Pacific Northwest—an area of the United States that includes Washington and Oregon

predators—animals that hunt other animals for food

rodents—small animals that gnaw on their food

scavengers—animals that eat food that is already dead

slash—to cut

solitary—living alone

tundra—dry land where the ground is frozen year-round

To Learn More

AT THE LIBRARY
Carr, Aaron. *Wolverine*. New York, N.Y.: AV2 by
Weigl, 2016.

O'Mara, John. *Wolverines*. New York, N.Y.: Gareth
Stevens Publishing, 2015.

Polinsky, Paige V. *Wolverine: Powerful Predator*.
Minneapolis, Minn.: Abdo Publishing, 2017.

ON THE WEB
Learning more about
wolverines is as easy as 1, 2, 3.

1. Go to www.factsurfer.com.

2. Enter "wolverines" into the search box.

3. Click the "Surf" button and you will see a
   list of related web sites.

With factsurfer.com, finding more
information is just a click away.

Index